GOD SAVE THE QUEEN

First published in 1981
by Clement (Publishers) Ltd.
34 Middleton Road, London E8 4BS

Printed by A. G. Bishop & Sons,
Orpington, Kent

ISBN 0 907027 03 2

British Library Cataloguing in Publication Data
Loveridge, John
God save the Queen: sonnets of Elizabeth I.
I. Title
821'. 914 PR6062.08/

GOD SAVE THE QUEEN
Sonnets of Elizabeth I

by
John Loveridge

Clement Publishers

INTRODUCTION

The story of Elizabeth's life has always been touched by an air of mystery. This is partly because she deliberately clouded her own actions to help her secret diplomacy; and also because her history has been confused by those historians whose prejudices, on one side or other of the great religious struggles, have left different pictures behind them. In part, too, it arises because whilst so much of the advice given to her by members of her government remains with us in written form, the views that she herself formed and upon which all action by the state was based, were kept as she herself might have expressed it 'in her own taciturnity'.

When Elizabeth came to the throne, England was weak. Fisher writes in his *History of Europe*: 'It was an open question whether the country would become a satellite of France or Spain'. Three problems threatened the end of the realm: Probable civil war over religion; defeat as a minor ally of Spain in the unsuccessful war against France and Scotland; and an increasing debt threatening ruin. How, from these uncertain foundations, did Elizabeth create the golden age of English history? Much of the answer lies in Elizabeth's own mind and it is in the ambitious hope of seeking some of the truth of this mind that these Sonnets are written. It is too late for Elizabeth to leave us her autobiography. I can only hope that she herself would not only have liked the Sonnets, but would feel that they represented some of her most heartfelt thoughts, both private and public, towards the great crises of her life and her realm.

The Sonnets start at an age when Elizabeth can speak for herself. What of her childhood? Elizabeth had been brought up searching for love among the succession of Henry VIII's Queens. Her own mother, Anne Boleyn, had been executed for the alleged treason of adultery with five men including her brother; Jane Seymour had died bearing the future King, Edward VI; Anne of Cleves had come and gone, quietly pensioned off; Catherine Howard had had one lover too many and so she too had been beheaded; and Katherine Parr, with whom Elizabeth continued to live after Henry's death in 1547, soon remarried only to die after childbirth late in the following year. The dangers of love in one form or another must have been only too apparent to the young princess.

Elizabeth was a child of the reformation in more senses than one. Before she was born, Henry had struggled for years with the Pope to obtain a divorce from his first wife, Catherine of Aragon, who had not produced a male heir. It was when Anne Boleyn become pregnant that Henry married her against the Pope's ruling. Thus it was Elizabeth's conception in her mother's womb that caused the final break of England from Rome. The princess was schooled in the latest learning as well as being taught the disputes of older days. She was proud to be a scholar and as she put it herself long after, 'I am more afraid of making a fault in my Latin than of the Kings of Spain, France, Scotland, the House of Guise and all their confederates!' Indeed, when Queen she seldom needed an interpreter to speak with the leading foreign visitors and ambassadors to whom she often spoke without intermediaries. She made certain that the judgements of English foreign policy and the actions upon them lay within her own hands. A French ambassador to the young Queen, who at first thought her foolish, was within months to write home in admiration of her dissimulation 'She is the best hand at the game living.' In England, she succeeded in holding the lifelong trust and loyal service of her principal ministers.

Opposite each poem is printed a brief background of history.

John Loveridge

This book is dedicated to my wife Jenny and to our children Amanda, Michael, Emma, Steven and Robert.

Acknowledgements

Frontispiece	Elizabeth I	by courtesy of the National Portrait Gallery, London

The Picture Gallery (pp i-xvi)

i	The Shield of Elizabeth I	
ii	Elizabeth I as Princess	reproduced by Gracious Permission of Her Majesty the Queen
iii	Thomas Seymour	by courtesy of the National Portrait Gallery, London
iv	Henry VIII	from the private collection of the author
v	Anne Boleyn	by courtesy of the National Portrait Gallery, London
vi	Lady Jane Grey	by courtesy of the National Portrait Gallery, London
vii	Mary I	from the private collection of the author
viii, ix	Launch of Fireships on the Armada at Gravelines	The National Maritime Museum, London
x	Sir John Hawkins	The National Maritime Museum, London
xi	Robert Dudley, First Earl of Leicester	by courtesy of the National Portrait Gallery, London
xii	First Baron Burghley	by courtesy of the National Portrait Gallery, London
xiii	Mary, Queen of Scots	by courtesy of the National Portrait Gallery, London
xiv	Robert Devereux, Second Earl of Essex	by courtesy of the National Portrait Gallery, London
xv	Robert Cecil, First Earl of Salisbury	by courtesy of the National Portrait Gallery, London
xvi	Elizabeth I	from the private collection of the author

I should like to say how grateful I am to my secretary, Mandi Jenkins, for her help in the preparation of this book and also to my publisher, Lionel Stanbrook, for all the trouble he has taken.

THE TUDORS

HENRY VII	Born 28 July 1457 Died 21 April 1509	Reigned 1485 - 1509
HENRY VIII	Born 28 June 1491 Died 28 January 1547	Reigned 1509 - 1547
EDWARD VI	Born 12 October 1537 (Henry VIII's son by Jane Seymour) Died 6 July 1553	Reigned 1547 - 1553
MARY I	Born 18 February 1516 (Henry VIII's daughter by Catherine of Aragon. Married Philip of Spain) Died 17 November 1558	Reigned 1553 - 1558
ELIZABETH I	Born 7 September 1533 (Henry VIII's daughter by Anne Boleyn) Died 24 March 1603	Reigned 1558 - 1603

Lady Jane Grey was Queen for nine days
from 10 July to 19 July 1553

GOD SAVE THE QUEEN
Sonnets of Elizabeth I

Sir Thomas Seymour, the brother of Jane, Henry VIII's third wife, was the Lord Admiral of England. This ambitious man was attracted by Elizabeth before he married Henry's Dowager Queen, Katherine Parr. It was his first marriage and her fourth. Elizabeth continued to live with Katherine.

The Admiral at times appeared in Elizabeth's bedroom to tickle her before she got up. At Whitsun, 1548, Katherine caught her husband with Elizabeth in his arms and sent the 14 year-old girl away to live elsewhere. Katherine died in September of that year, lingering a week after childbirth.

The Lord Admiral plotted against his brother (the Duke of Somerset) who was the Lord Protector, ruling England during the childhood of Edward VI. The plots were discovered, he was arrested in January and executed on the 20th March, 1549.

ELIZABETH TO SEYMOUR

My Lord it is a dangerous game you play
        To touch a Princess with these lover's hands.
Thy head is ransom for a heart today
        Which may not wish to rule these England lands.

Make not these royal clothes in disarray,
        For here no Tudor passion shall unbend,
Nor daring trust lead caution to obey,
        And give assuagement to a sailor's whim.

What does my own Lord Admiral intend?
        The swift exchange of kiss for kiss, or more?
Guard well the blood in which a peer may swim!
        Cousin, take this last touch, and close the score.

I may remember him upon the throne
If ever we shall reign: Queen, alone.

– 1548 –

If Elizabeth, as a contingent heir to the throne, had been thinking of marriage with Seymour after his wife's death, there might be a case against her for treason if she had not asked permission of the Lord Protector and the Council. Sir Robert Tyrwhit, who interrogated her for the Council, wrote 'by no way will she confess... concerning my Lord Admiral and yet I do see it in her face that she is guilty.' Elizabeth admitted nothing and the suspicious Council finally accepted her innocence of any conspiracy to marry. After this Elizabeth wisely appeared to be a pious and sensible girl, working hard at her studies.

THE PROTECTOR'S PRISONER

I love my Lord. My Lord will die. I dared
To blush upon his name: now to myself
Must see. No tears, nor fear, nor this heart bared
Shall any know but I my guarding self.

I am not marred by love: fear I instead
To feel that pausing chill; the gentle lip
Of death's appraisal kiss my golden head.
Oh entrail's pain! Tongue may not make one slip.

Stay Sir, the Council's peace I'll not disturb:
All I confess, for all is none. I had
No hope to wed but on their sanctioned word.
I would not otherwise if I were sad,

Instead I gladly read in Duty's book
And each page open for my Lords to look.

– 1549 –

The Duke of Northumberland had succeeded the Duke of Somerset as leader of the Council, and Somerset had been executed for treason. The young king, Edward VI, was ill with tuberculosis and, in his zeal for a Protestant succession, had named Lady Jane Grey in his will as the heir to the throne. Lady Jane, who was married to Northumberland's son, was declared Queen by the Council four days after the young king's death.

The king's health must have deteriorated suddenly. His death appears to have caught Northumberland by surprise since neither Mary nor Elizabeth were in his hands at the time. Northumberland sent for the sisters. Elizabeth is said to have been saved by a friend who warned her after she had set out on the road to London. Mary also escaped the men sent for her and took up arms. The Protector's own army sent to seize her deserted to Mary and she became Queen in July 1553. Northumberland was executed for treason but mercy was initially shown to Lady Jane, Queen for nine days, and to her husband.

MARY TUDOR, QUEEN

My brother dead: bring not such news to me.
  He asked to see my face; my picture sent;
I wrote my letter, which he could not see?
  In March last year we met: The Arab tent

Moves place to place. Nomads the deserts know:
  My place is kept. The King I visit would,
But was turned back upon the road. The slow
  Approach to death has not turned back. Who should

Be Queen? My Lord Protector asks me there.
  I think it best to stay. Which Queen is made?
Mary by my father's will is heir.
  God numb me that I do not fall. The shade

I seek. Is luck my only Council now?
Oh sister, Queen, to thee I'm glad to bow.

– 1553 –

Mary's bethrothal to a foreign and Catholic king, Philip of Spain, led to a plot against her under the leadership of Sir Thomas Wyatt. Captured and imprisoned, Wyatt under torture implicated Elizabeth, but when he came to the scaffold, he declared her innocent of complicity in any plot.

Elizabeth was arrested. She asked Mary to see her. She was refused and wrote a letter pleading to be seen whilst the barge that was to take her to the Tower lay waiting. In the letter Elizabeth reminds her sister that the former Lord Protector, the Duke of Somerset, had been heard to say after the execution of his brother, Thomas Seymour, that if only he had seen him he might have spared his brother's life.

Lady Jane Grey and her husband were now executed, but no proof of any treason had been found against Elizabeth. She was released from the Tower and sent to live at Woodstock under restraint, where she proved a fierce prisoner resistant to petty rules and restrictions.

After Mary's marriage to Philip of Spain, Elizabeth was allowed to attend the Court. There, at a time when Mary was burning many Protestants at the stake for heresy in her zeal to restore the Catholic faith in England, Elizabeth, after some demur, wisely attended Mass.

BY THE THAMES: ON THE STEPS
TO THE TOWER

In this same place my mother knelt before.
    Noble Lords of Sussex and of Winchester,
Should I pay forfeit for another's score?
    I never feared uphold the Queen, my sister:

I am her heir of this our English throne;
    She has my fealty. Say this to her:
My heart no treason knows; the Queen alone
    Is here my guardian, and none dare swear,

Except in torments' lies, drawn from the rack,
    That any choice could make this subject less
Than hers. I saw ambition's almanack
    Two brothers past divide; would I distress

My sovereign for so dear exchange? Oh see
This Thames accepts my tears, see loyalty.

– 1554 –

21

Mary thought that she was with child. Instead, it was death growing within her. She died on 17th November, 1558. After his wife's death, Philip thought that he could influence the new Queen Elizabeth, but after years of discretion to save her life, Elizabeth was ready to reign on her own.

What was Elizabeth's inheritance? England was a nation of small size and little strength, a minor ally of Spain in an unsuccessful war against France. Calais, that outpost for defence and trade, had fallen, 'engraved on Mary's heart' when she died, and French troops were dominant in Scotland. The English numbered 4 millions, the French 16 millions, and the Spanish peoples 12 millions. The Northern Dutch, later to play a great part in the story, were some 2 million strong.

Elizabeth knew by simple arithmetic that these figures necessitated a policy of brains not brawn for survival. Time and time again she was to over-rule her enthusiastic advisors when they forgot these essential facts of national life. Peace was made with France but the threat remained 'the French King bestriding the realm, having one foot in Calais and the other in Scotland'. In 1560, the French were driven from Scotland forever and in future English national policy could indeed be as Elizabeth said of herself 'mere English'.

In spite of the costs of the war Elizabeth soon established herself as credit-worthy, and in later years could borrow more cheaply from international bankers than any of her more powerful rivals. She reformed the coinage to stop inflation, and more important, she reformed the Church.

GOD SAVE THE QUEEN

The fires die down: the babe not born, the end,
    And Calais gone. You say that I am Queen?
Then pray with me: 'Dear God, good guidance send'.
    Dry thou for me the first tear of your Queen.

Who sets the feast? Around me so much thirst
    I see. The wine myself must choose, and in
This Court as well, the Fool. Come, quench that thirst
    With me. I shall good measure give. Old sin

Is past, and fame awaits in Virtue's shade.
    Once I myself was touched by sun when young.
I fled to safer shade. Now light be made,
    And hear us all the songs of England sung.

Come, play with me upon our English stage:
Come, write with me on History's waiting page.

-1558-

After Mary I died many exiled Protestants started to return to England. Foxe's Book of Martyrs had inflamed Protestant England but Elizabeth was determined not to get into the hands of either a Calvinist party or a Catholic party. It was Elizabeth's genius to see that this was no case for a policy of 'divide and rule'. She chose instead unity and control. She wanted one Church, as broad as possible, to ensure a united nation. Most of Mary's clergy, though not the Bishops, were content to continue in their livings under Elizabeth, and for ten years there was peace from religious strife in England.

OF CHRIST AND HIS APOSTLES' LAW

Death's shadow strengthened me when young: dear God
Shall I then fear to pray? Good Chaucer spoke
Of Christ and His apostles' law: One God,
One land, one Church and neither hate nor yoke

Permit. No burnings for the Papal See,
Nor monies for a foreign Prince. Nor Calvin's
Pre-determined horrors here. Clergy:
I do not wish to know soul's secret sins,

One Church may hold in peace each private view.
Old temples and old gods have gone before.
Unite, then each good voice of God is true,
And I will ask no more from Church or Law.

Dear God: I truly pray this heart to Thee,
And thankful am for our protecting sea.

– 1559 –

Elizabeth had fallen in love with Lord Robert Dudley (later to be created Earl of Leicester). They had known each other since childhood and had both been imprisoned in the Tower at the same time. Robert was a son of the former Protector, Northumberland. Some of the Queen's Council were alarmed at this romance as Dudley was already married. It seems likely that although they were lovers they never consummated their affection. Perhaps they spoke of divorce. Amy, Dudley's wife, was ill and thought by some to be dying. Perhaps Elizabeth and Dudley hoped to be married in the future, but events conspired to make this an impossible dream. In the end, Elizabeth preferred to remain the virgin Queen.

ELIZABETH TO LEICESTER

Love thee I do, as much indeed I dare.
    Dear Robin, love, could I but love you half
So much, and that be love too great. We care
    Our duty, you and I, beyond this path

Of hearts' dement. We steal our kisses, love
    For love, not from this English throne, or all
I am were yours; but from our larger love:
    This yeoman land. And so it seems the call

Of Nature's own sweet choice is out of tune
    Or I would kiss and never let you go:
Perhaps command you now to storm the moon,
    And laugh to find the waking sunrise glow.

Not so: pledge I am England's wife alone,
'Sweet eyes', and shall reign on from this brave throne.

– 1560 –

Elizabeth loved Robert for life. In 1562 she may have secretly hoped to be able to marry him. His wife, Amy (née Robsart) was said to be suffering from cancer, and was thought to be dying. Unfortunately, the wife, having let all her staff go off to a fair for the day, was found dead on their return at the foot of a flight of stairs with her neck broken. Enemies alleged murder. A jury found the death accidental but Elizabeth must surely have felt that she could never have married Dudley after this accident, because it could only endanger the throne due to the circumstances surrounding his wife's death.

Suicide had been ruled out because her clothes were little disturbed, as might have been expected after a long fall. It is now known that some forms of cancer weaken the bone structure and it is possible that Amy merely slipped on the last few steps, and that this was enough to break the weak bones.

Dudley retained Elizabeth's highest respect and when, in the same year, she thought that she herself was dying with smallpox, she recommended him to her Council as Protector and declared 'nothing improper had ever passed between them'.

Elizabeth lost much of her hair but her face was largely spared. Robert's beautiful sister, who nursed her, caught the disease and was so badly pock-marked that she became a recluse and would not appear at Court again.

ON HEARING OF LADY DUDLEY'S DEATH

Some say that she was ill and soon to die;
  I can believe it so without your love.
Oh what anguish in that mortal cry,
  Called to seek assuagement, nearer God, above.

So gone she be: my rival for your kiss.
  Some would accuse; of envy and of greed:
They say your hand, our hand, was touched in this;
  That we in murder might fulfil our need.

I know you well. Your presence here shows all
  Of my belief, yet we must prove you free
Of doubt. Men true in mind shall test that fall,
  Fatal to her; and fatal too for me,

Who never now, for England's hopes, may wed.
We are defeated by the poor, poor, dead.

– 1562 –

Parliament after parliament pressed Elizabeth to marry so that there might be an heir for the future safety of England and the religious settlement. So long as the Catholics saw Mary of Scotland as the direct heir to Elizabeth there continued a natural expectation for a Catholic succession to the throne. Equally, Catholics could still hope that Elizabeth might marry a Catholic prince. If, however, she married a Protestant and had a child, in this new situation there would be a strong motive for Elizabeth's assassination, but one cannot help feeling that she might have set such considerations aside to marry Robert Dudley if the circumstances of his wife's death had not been such a barrier. She created him Earl of Leicester in 1564.

Elizabeth must have been lonely in the palaces in which she lived. She never allowed one courtier, or a group of courtiers, to control her action. She spoke singly to each and kept their trust. She flirted with many men which helped her to lure their confidences, but at the same time, she kept her own counsel and rapped their knuckles if necessary when they attempted to infringe on her prerogative to rule.

ON MARRIAGE

Think not that I my father's daughter am?
    Lust I not for the very kiss of love?
Steal my heart: take the childless pram.
    Stroke soft the feathers of the dewy dove!

Press into my bosom: touch desire.
    Lips are my memory: strength my hope,
Yet may a Princess leap with bodies fire!
    One Queen, may never, virgin, once elope.

Think that I should be wedded, choose to die,
    When spoused be I to this our English land?
A king could think a wife he might defy:
    Should I swop England for a golden band?

My passion is: so let it life-time be:
I am of England: say, so married she!

– 1565 –

31

Mary, Queen of Scots, was the natural heir to Elizabeth's throne, through descent from her grandmother Margaret, a sister of Henry VIII. Mary, as a Catholic, was not looked forward to as Queen by the Protestant parliament of England.

The English had held Mary since her escape from Scotland in May 1568. The Scots wanted their Queen back to try her for the murder of her husband. Elizabeth held her in England rather than force her to return to trial and almost certain death. The two Queens never met. Elizabeth wrote 'When you are acquitted of this crime I will receive you with all honour: till that is done I may not.'

Mary was the natural centre of Catholic plots against Elizabeth, and in November 1569, some leading Catholics marched in rebellion from Durham after the years of peace at home. They were encouraged to rebel by the success of the Catholic cause against the Huguenots in France. The rebellion, led by the Northern Lords, Thomas Percy, Earl of Northumberland, and Charles Neville, Earl of Westmorland, was soon defeated, and many of the old Catholics remained loyal to Elizabeth.

In 1570, but too late to help the rebellion, Elizabeth was excommunicated by the Pope and 'deprived of her pretended right to the realm'. This led to increasing legislation against Roman Catholics and in time was to be taken as an absolution by those intending to murder Elizabeth. Even so Elizabeth continued her policy of refusing to become leader of the Protestants in Europe. Her foreign policy was based on the belief that in most instances national self-interest would prove a stronger force amongst rulers than religion.

ON THE NORTHERN REBELLION

Let Mary die they say. Not I who grew
    Among such blooded hands. Not I, unless
I must. Meantime of Percy and the few,
    Who with Westmorland must still confess

Their trespass to a band of priests: Permit
    Of treason once; and once were twice enough,
So crush rebellion where its seed may set.
    For landlords, treason is a foolish bluff,

And when their blooded fields are sown again
    Those lands shall have more value than their heads.
The sun will surely ripen next year's grain
    And if reluctant rebels seek their beds,

And hide their swords, our half-closed eyes may turn
Away. We wish no flesh, for souls, to burn.

On the eve of St Bartholomew's Feast, 1572, thousands of Huguenots had gathered in Paris for celebrations following a royal marriage between the Catholic Marguerite of Valois, sister to Charles IX, King of France, and the young Protestant Henry, King of Navarre, who lived on and later became Henry IV, King of France. Instead of reconciliation, the Medici Queen Mother and the King, her son, started a slaughter and very few Huguenots escaped, including the children. The killings spread to the provinces and led to the fourth war of religion in France. There were seven such wars during Elizabeth's lifetime.

It was perhaps as well that Parliament was not sitting or Elizabeth's vital alliance with France, signed only that April, might have been jeopardized by the outcry of outraged public opinion. As it was, an angry Elizabeth was said to have received the French Ambassador at her court, lined up in silence and in full mourning.

Elizabeth, though, was more than anxious to offset the threat of Spain through her alliance with France. The Spanish power had enormously increased since their defeat of the Turks in the decisive naval battle of Lepanto a year before. Even so, Spain would not wish to take on both France and England at once. Elizabeth, therefore, maintained her alliance with France, one result of which was that when the Spanish Armada came many years later, it was unable to enter the deep water port of Calais which might have saved the Spaniards from the fireships and storms that destroyed them.

ELIZABETH RECEIVES THE
FRENCH AMBASSADOR
AFTER HEARING OF THE
MASSACRE OF ST BARTHOLOMEW'S EVE

Paris, city of cities, Charles the host
 Of many the hopeful thousand wedding guests!
Sang they of love: raised for Christ His Host?
 What hands of horror bare the vampired breasts?

Old friends cut down, and the children struck to die.
 Of what Medici magic this? What touch
The killing fingers felt? What insane cry
 Commands such deeds? Grew this from fearing much?

What small child's entrails guard a frightened king?
 What doctrine had the slaughtered babes to teach?
What little eyes were plucked? Whose regal ring
 The setting for such jewels? That hand shall reach

To make our new alliance firm: pray just
Ensure your mistress knows, we share her trust.

– 1572 –

The sixteenth century was an age of cruelty in sport. Bear-baiting and cock-fighting were national entertainments. At tournaments in the tilt yards knights still sometimes wounded each other, even though their lances were blunted. The Queen muses on the reasons for her own harshness to a deer whose life she had spared after a hunt, but whose ears were cut off as a ransom. This is said to have happened at Leicester's castle of Kenilworth in the county of Warwickshire.

As time went by Elizabeth felt forced to act against extremists who brought danger to the fabric of the state. Two men from a Calvinist sect of Anabaptists, that had come over from the Netherlands, were condemned for heresy and burned in 1577. Although Catholics were never condemned for their private exercise of religion they were required to conform publicly, and the law was tightened against them after the rebellion of 1569 and even more during the long war with Spain. The first execution of a Jesuit priest who had entered the country from abroad came in 1579. This after he was condemned for treason, not for heresy. After 1584 the foreign trained priests were required by Act of Parliament to leave the country.

AT KENILWORTH: ON THE
MANAGEMENT OF MEN

We each are small, yet dare not show this face:
  Men long so much to climb, to take some fort
For so much blood: Or seize some throne,
  Great store or might: All place least on 'ought

To do'. At Kenilworth I cut two ears
  From some sweet deer when caught; and let it live.
I laughed, and knew that they who heard had ears
  To hear, and eyes to see what Queens may give.

Sane cruelty: handmaiden of our crown!
  Lose you and we lose all. The souls of men
Are better taught: My softest kiss, my frown
  In sharp antithesis: My love and then

Dear children for your good, the sugared bite,
That keeps the bitter sweet. Arise Sir Knight!

– 1574 –

37

Elizabeth accepted John Hawkins' view, against much opposition, that the Royal Navy's ships should be built for their sailing qualities, and their broadsides used to sink their enemies. In the event, it was not easy to sink large galleons at long range but, even so, the sailing qualities of the Queen's ships and their harassing fire proved too much for the great galleons of Spain.

The Spanish policy was to bring their large vessels alongside so that their famous soldiers, supported by a crew of few sailors, could board the enemy. Their sailing qualities, however, were unequal to those of the English ships, manned almost entirely by sailors.

In 1577 Francis Drake took three small ships to raid Spanish possessions and in the process not only circumnavigated the world but also proved that Spain's powerful empire could be penetrated effectively. Elizabeth's share of the booty he brought home amounted to £160,000, nearly as much as half a year of her ordinary income to finance the country. After his three years at sea Drake was knighted by Elizabeth on the deck of his own ship, the Golden Hind. Elizabeth took with her the French Ambassador to demonstrate her alliance with France for defence against Spain and, before dubbing Sir Francis, she joked that the sword might remove his head!

ELIZABETH TO HAWKINS: ON EQUIPPING THE NAVY

These ships, my Master Hawkins, you assure
    Me are the best. Elsewhere we hear not so.
For costs so great we should at least be sure.
    Thin and long, deep of draught, and low,

With longer guns designed to hit and run.
    But can you sink with culverins like these?
Might not great galleons sail too close, and stun
    You with their soldiers high above your crews?

We have not men for soldiering at sea
    And must therefore rely on new ideas:
So place our stake upon artillery
    Of brass, and chance your arm against our fears.

Invention has its place in war: we wait
The premised proving of your plans; our Fate.

– 1578 –

Elizabeth always wanted to ensure that the deep water ports of the Lowlands and Calais were either in English hands, or in friendly hands. Some Catholics and the Guise family in France tried to draw France into a Catholic League of alliance with Spain against whom the Netherlands were in rebellion. Elizabeth's policy was to fend off Spain without actually coming to war with this much more powerful and larger country.

The increasing militancy of English private shipping can in part be seen by the search for new markets to replace those that had been closed against England's exports largely due to the fighting and unrest in the Netherlands. Elizabeth, however, refused to allow her own fleets to go too far afield, both to keep the crews from scurvy and to ensure that they were near enough to meet any attack on England.

ELIZABETH TO BURGHLEY:
ON STRATEGY

The Dutch we pay, send troops to if we must,
    The French, against the League, we shall support:
First Henry of Navarre, and then the King,
    Whose civil wars and neutral place may make

The Spaniard pause. Philip we show our strength
    On far off seas, and take a profit from
Our pirateers. The Scots we would align
    With our affairs, yet fear their former Queen,

Our heir, whom we would recognise, if trust
    We could. Our strength lies in our trade. Our ships
Protect it, and our land. When fleets we must
    Provision, keep those close by Southern shore,

On monthly stocks, careened, thus fresh for health,
And close in my control against alarm.

– 1580 –

In 1582 the 'cold' war was going badly. Portugal had fallen to Spain two years before and Philip's new commander in the Netherlands, the Duke of Parma, within months of his arrival, had brought the southern or Belgian provinces largely back to their Spanish allegiance.

Cambrai was besieged. Elizabeth wanted French troops committed against Parma. Henry III of France in effect replied: marry my brother, the Duc d'Alençon, and we will fight together. He would not fight with Spain if England might back out. (In fact d'Alençon had been Duc d'Anjou since 1574 but is better known by his earlier title.)

Elizabeth welcomed a formal betrothal, but wrote six weeks' delay into the marriage contract. Henry's brother, whom Elizabeth playfully termed her 'Frog', seemed sure of the marriage and with money from Elizabeth 15,000 men were gathered to relieve the siege. With the troops engaged in July, Elizabeth deferred the marriage declaring 'though her body was hers, her soul was wholly his'. The French army entered Cambrai in August, and Elizabeth had to pay in hard cash as a palliative to France.

During the marriage negotiations, the Queen must have been sorely tempted to go through with the marriage to d'Alençon, for the French Ambassador carefully told her what no one else had dared, that her beloved Robin (Earl of Leicester) had secretly married Lettice Knowles, when she was seven months' pregnant, some four years earlier in September 1578.

DEPARTURE OF THE FROG

Alone I dream, for Princes dare not trust.
    Dear Frog you played my part. Who cheated you?
My island home, or I? If only lust
    Could be enough! Loved Robin wed, then who

Am I, with each remembered hope consumed?
    Go playful Frog, French soldiers earned your crown,
But I'll not pay the debt French pride assumed;
    Nor weep again upon my Robin's frown,

Nor ask for much. My heart is hurt. Depart!
    One empty womb: all faithless lovers flown.
One empty room: just England and my heart
    Alone, as all true princes' hearts, alone.

Go tell the Dutch their safety I have charmed,
To pluck an army from your loving arms!

– 1582 –

The Spanish had reinforced their armies in the Lowlands and even the great city of Antwerp fell to them in August 1585. Elizabeth decided to intervene directly and in December an English army left for the Netherlands under Lord Leicester's command.

Elizabeth did not wish to claim sovereignty of soil owned by Spain, as the Netherlands then was. She feared that this would involve her in open war with Spain, yet she had to sustain the rebels to prevent the Spaniards from regaining their ports, which were not only vital for English trade, but were also centres from which any attack on England could be launched.

Leicester was instructed not to accept regal status, but it was difficult to get the Dutch to risk their soldiers in a joint command unless they were sure that the English would never quit and leave them in the lurch. Elizabeth had previously insisted that the ports of Flushing and Brill were in English hands in exchange for her loans of money to sustain the Dutch in their rebellion against Spain.

INSTRUCTIONS FOR THE DUTCH WAR

The Dutch at war plead to me for their lands:
    Offer me their crown. Should England wed
With Europe's soil? In Spain stooped Philip stands,
    And dreams to turn this way his Catholic head!

We fleece Spain's ships and pay the Dutch the spoil.
    Such actions will not turn to open war,
But place a sovereign claim on Philip's soil:
    The sizzling fuse will run to powder's store.

No title for such rule dare we accept!
    Within the confines of our purse take men,
Keep free the ports that should be safely kept,
    And then we may, perhaps, seek peace again.

Come, Robin, drum your soldiers through the town,
Yet still recall, I throw no gauntlet down.

– 1585 –

In February 1586, when Lord Leicester was in Holland, he accepted the title of Governor and Captain-General of the States. When the Queen heard this her anger was immense. She wrote at once 'we could never have imagined, had we not seen it fall out in experience, that a man raised up by ourself, and extraordinarily favoured by us above any subject of this land, would have in so contemptable a sort broken a commandment...' He was to give up the title. The letter ended on the ominous note 'whereof fail you not, as you will answer the contrary at your uttermost peril.' Elizabeth's temper was not improved by knowing that his wife was to join him.

In a few months her beloved Robin was forgiven. Lord Leicester came home from the Netherlands to command the English armies preparing for the expected invasion. Against Dutch protests he left English Catholics commanding two important posts, but for these two officers religion overcame patriotism. On the 28th January, 1587, they went over to the enemy taking with them over 1,000 men, and one declared 'before I served the Devil: now I serve God.' Elizabeth's old belief that most of her Catholic subjects would loyally support her was rudely shaken. The pressures on Elizabeth to act against Mary had been many and now she decided to act forthwith.

Year by year Jesuit priests had come into England to sustain remaining members of the old religion. Although many were more interested in faith than in politics they inevitably represented a danger to Elizabeth. The Cardinal Secretary at the Vatican had given a clear answer to the question of whether mortal sin would be incurred by Elizabeth's murder. 'There is no doubt whatsoever who sends her out of the world with the pious intention of doing God's service not only does not sin but gains merit.'

LORD LEICESTER DISOBEYS

Who bites my hand through this my gentle glove?
*   My heart is low, and jealous, angered much.*
From what I might not give she stole my love;
*   And my own Council plead my softer touch!*

Has England great resource to fight and fight?
*   Yet he who paid so much must make it so,*
His young wife Queening there. Dark of my night.
*   My love, old servant, fail thou whom? One show*

Of weakness: I command no more. Thus every great
*   Design upset; my daring balance falls*
To war with Spain. Should jealousy, strange fate,
*   A sovereign's mind confuse? What vain voice calls?*

But there is more than this. Know all of thee,
Lord Leicester shall obey, and bow to me.

– 1586 –

After all these years, Mary, Queen of Scots, was still held in England, well treated as Queen but still a prisoner. The English discovered that secret letters were being sent and received by her, hidden in the bung of a barrel. In one letter she encouraged a plot against Elizabeth's life: this was treason. After hesitating for months, on the 1st February 1587, Elizabeth signed the warrant for Mary's death. It seems likely she had just heard the bad news that her Catholic troops in Holland had gone over to the enemy three days earlier. The execution took place in the Great Hall of Fotheringhay on the 8th February. Mary was also the widow of a king of France. Would her death threaten the French alliance? Crowds in Paris roared for vengeance. Elizabeth showed immense anguish after the execution and denied that she had intended the death warrant to be carried out. She alleged that, although she had signed the warrant, Davidson, the new secretary in her Council, had exceeded his authority in getting together with the Privy Council to add the Great Seal to the document. Davidson was dismissed his post, but later given a good pension. In the event, France remained neutral.

Mary's death changed much. The succession was now assured to her son, James, King of Scotland, who had been brought up by the Calvinists and was now twenty years of age.

ELIZABETH REFLECTS ON HEARING
OF MARY'S EXECUTION

She was my heir. Her severed head they say
Was old and grey, and wigged: That Queen of France
And Scotland, who long dreamed to reign today
On England's throne. Courage she had. Her dance

Led men to die: her death may lead still more.
What was arranged is done. Our sorrow shows
Itself. Queens should not lightly die. The store
And show of our distress may keep the throws

Of anguish fresh before all governments.
What moves upon this news will Europe make?
Too many troops may strike their cantonments.
And for ourselves? At least we must ask Drake

To fleece (with our support obscure) and bleed
Those ships by Spanish shore. Oh this land we lead!

– 1587 –

The Spanish commander in the Netherlands, the Duke of Parma, was in difficulties because death among his soldiers had reduced his force from 30,000 to 17,000 men. In 1587, the port of Sluys had fallen to the Spaniards in spite of valiant efforts under Leicester to relieve the defenders. Here the Spaniards could collect shallow draft barges in which to carry their soldiers, but the junction of a Spanish fleet and the barges could not be achieved without a deep water port. These were held by the English or the neutral French.

Drake took a fleet to destroy ships assembling for the Armada in Spanish ports. Elizabeth kept all options open by sending a message cancelling the order to Drake, but made sure it arrived after he had already sailed. Drake's success delayed the Armada by a year. His destruction of the mature staves for making water casks ensured that when the Armada of 130 ships and 27,500 men did sail the new water casks warped and sprang leaks.

In 1588, the Armada sailed from Spain. The barges and soldiers in the Lowlands were made ready. The English fleet shepherded the Spaniards up the Channel and sent in fire ships late on the 28th July when the Armada was lying outside Calais. This led the Spaniards to cut their anchor cables in confusion. Then storms led them to sail to the North Sea. At home, where it was still thought that the invasion might be attempted without the protection of the Spanish fleet, Leicester commanded the main army which was gathered near Tilbury. Elizabeth reviewed 11,500 of her troops there on the 8th August. With Leicester was his young stepson, Robert Devereux. In the poem, Elizabeth reminds herself of her own famous speech to her army.

AFTER TILBURY

The feared Armada sailing on toward
    The Northern seas: Shall it return? I doubt.
Today I spoke at Tilbury: and even awed
    Our men! Loved men of mine; your turns about,

They vexed, I think your sergeants; and yet
    May vex the Spaniards more. What vengeance if
That thirsting fleet shall land! None shall forget
    The courage of these days. Robin, the stiff

Reward of duty is my love. Your stepson rode
    Near me; and my sons cheered ten thousand strong!
Enough of reminiscence here! The 'Toad'
    Of Spain hopes for my head; and is he wrong?

'Foul scorn', 'Let tyrants fear'. It's good and true;
We know well now what we, if needs, must do.

— 1588 —

51

In spite of Leicester's marriage he always remained very close to Elizabeth. After his death she treated his stepson, Robert, Earl of Essex, with exceptional favour. Elizabeth, however, refused ever to allow Leicester's wife into her presence or to come to the court during his lifetime. After the Queen's death, amongst a few of her precious trinkets, was found a letter from Leicester marked in her own hand 'his last letter'. He died on 4th September 1588.

ON LEICESTER'S DEATH

You were our hero, more than all. The rest
    Were part of policy. You had my heart,
My love, my hate; and yet remained life's zest,
    When you had sealed my loving, to depart.

Brave soldier, noble in the dearest cause
    Of England's name; we set you first, and last,
Where time obliterates at length these wars
    Of man's estate. Oh God, must past be past?

No more to see this ageing man. This soul
    Should weep, should die. They say he spoke of me,
But I am chilled, and Robin cold.
    So rusts another nail in England's Tree.

My ladies! Here! Ask Burghley's presence. Pray,
Are there no good despatches for the day?

– 1588 –

A year after the Armada the English counter-attacked taking a fleet of 150 ships and 18,000 men in an attempt to seize Portugal from Spain's rule but the expedition failed through heavy loss of life from sickness.

The long war went on: increasingly Englishmen reached out in offensive operations overseas. In spite of the richness of commercial life at home, Elizabeth found it difficult to finance the war. She had always courted the popularity of her people by policies of low taxation. Even so, monopoly interests, granted to members of her government, led to public complaints. Each year brought its toll of death from actions fought half across the world, as well as in Europe. England was learning to live in conditions of permanent war.

Philip prepared new fleets for invasion, and in 1596, a surprise attack captured Calais before the English could respond to Henry IV's appeal for help. Again, the English destroyed the shipping in Cadiz but Philip still managed to dispatch an invasion fleet that October. It suffered severe losses and turned back in the face of heavy gales. As one of Elizabeth's bishops once cried out 'God is an Englishman'.

The great war continued throughout Elizabeth's life. Burghley was now her chief Councillor. He had been a member of her Council since her succession over thirty years before, and was getting old. Elizabeth was forced to look for younger men to help with the business of government. Burghley's son, Robert Cecil, was brought into the government and so was Leicester's stepson, Robert Devereux, Second Earl of Essex. This ambitious nobleman was jealous that his own appointment came after that of Cecil. He thought that his military fame and the aristocracy of his family should give him first place. The Puritans thought of him as the 'swordsman of God'.

TO THE DEAD OF ENGLISH WAR

All beauty gone: farewell. Do heroes weep?
　　Watch they from heaven us at home parade?
We dream of them, those dead that take our sleep:
　　We do not give them more. In what sick shade

They wait until at last they lonely die?
　　Weep we for those dread sweethearts ever more?
How soon, so far from wounds' decay, our cry
　　No answered echo hears from graveyard shore?

Sands wash the blood-stained beaches clean, and we
　　Maintain our fierce pursuit of war. Those cherished
Dead, like counters moved on maps, were free
　　To fall. And here, where dreams lie dead, what anguished

Lips, fierce loving burned before, now turn
Along new regiments to kiss and learn?

- 1594 -

The Queen's government always wished to negotiate a peace safe for England. At the last Council meeting attended by the aged Lord Burghley, the only commoner to whom Elizabeth gave a peerage, the old man placed a Bible into the hands of Essex and touching the text said 'men of blood shall not live out half their days'. When a little time later Burghley lay dying, in 1598, the Queen fed him with a spoon from her own hand.

AND WITH INEXORABLE TIME

As Princes fade their power declines. Is this
    The view of those whose romanced words I hear?
Raleigh and the rest: they speak to kiss,
    Flatter these ageing hands. Spare they one tear

Against the truth of my unmirrored face?
    The love I bore them all was true. We reign
With love's delights where fearing tyrants trace
    Their fall and, Tudor, I shall rule the same

Whilst these old sinews clasp to prey upon
    The passing of old friends. Some dare to say
We should have care of flesh. Old comrades gone,
    Would you have spoken so? Am I too gay

For these young men? Is England ageing so?
    It was not thus, of savants and grim men,
We made our country to these riches grow.
    Queens to survive should show the strength of ten:

Ten little men! Where shall I find just one
    For primogeniture? All nations wait.
I too. England, my love, indeed my son,
    I wish for you that I might strengthen fate.

They say old women talk too much. Are longer
    Verses sign of this? Think well ye few:
I am not ready yet to let you ponder
    On a Scotsman to replace your shrew!

When I shall go, dear land, thou art alone
And must survive like all sweet fledglings flown.

– 1600 –

Essex was a brave and able leader, exceptionally favoured by the Queen. It is possible that the Queen thought him to be a natural son of the Earl of Leicester. The first Lord Essex had been deeply suspicious of his wife, Lettice, when her son, Robert, was born in 1566, and was said to show 'a very cold conceit' to the boy, though giving much affection to his second son. Leicester and Lettice were married two years after her husband's death.

Essex was sent to take command of the war in Ireland, with the greatest powers ever conferred on an Irish deputy. Even these he exceeded, over-ruling direct orders from the Queen. He made a truce with the Irish rebels but was forbidden to grant terms, after which he hastened to London, entering without warning the Queen's bedroom in Nonsuch Palace. Although she was not fully dressed, she talked kindly with the dangerous intruder. Next day he was imprisoned. Said Elizabeth, 'I am no Queen! That man is above me!' When released from prison he gathered a mixed group of adventurers who planned to seize the Queen. The small rebellion was soon overcome. Most were pardoned but Essex was executed. He was 34 years old.

ELIZABETH TO ESSEX

Your natural father (thought perhaps to be)
    My truant boy, I wished in you and sought
To see. My heir you think? My Chief could be?
    Brave man; not son of us, that which you ought

To be. We watched you grow, gave weapons to
    Your reaching hand; kissed that fine brow. We met
In gentle love; and now shall bid adieu.
    Not long, dear son; pretending we forget
Your profaned words, but wait the morning dew

That on our graves shall lie. When may I hold
    Your hand again; forgiveness give, and take?
Young Cecil sit with me this while: We scold
    Your learning's worth, yet value it. (The ache
Of this tired heart, alas, prefers the bold).

My dear Lord Essex dead? Who asks of Queens
So much? What actor needs to play such scenes?

– 1601 –

The Queen delighted in encouraging the use of men's minds. Literature reached heights not known since classical times. Almost every town had a grammar school. A humane system of help for the poor was established as a corporate duty of society. The power of England had risen from weakness to greatness, but at the State Opening of Elizabeth's last Parliament in 1601 the Queen sank under the weight of her robes, to be caught and held up. In a great but modest speech the Queen granted freedom from monopolies and truly said 'There is no jewel, be it of never so rich a price, which I set before this jewel: I mean your love.'

MY DRESS IS WORN

Oh let me be! I am no dreamer, but
    Of doing made. And I have done enough:
Life's long adventures truly loved: pray shut
    Away adventure for a day. The stuff

Of sinews weakens. Fails the driven heart.
    Oh let me be! No more the same sleep I.
One sweetmeat sleep of silence and we part.
    Another dream or two before we fly?

My dress is worn, my smock is touched by stain.
    Oft beside the still lake's shore I hear
The melodies of old songs sung again.
    Who hears those notes that shall not spring a tear?

Yet I am Queen: Queen, who rules in me?
What sap drives upwards through this gnarled tree?

– 1602 –

The Christmas of 1602 was spent dancing at Whitehall. Temperate eating and drinking and the Queen's indomitable spirit had carried her through to her seventieth year. Her height of five foot three inches was stooped and frail but she always acted as if she had years to reign, although she was sad when her coronation ring had to be filed from her rheumatic hand. She had always suffered headaches from much poring over books, but seldom spoke of her pains. Even so she had increasing spells of melancholy and sleepless nights.

Elizabeth caught a cold in January, and then moved to Richmond Palace, wearing summer clothes in an exceptionally sharp season. It became hard for her to swallow or speak. On the 19th March, Robin Carey, a relative, wrote to James VI in Scotland that the Queen could not last three days. Cecil told her 'Madam, to content the people, you must go to bed.' The Queen smiled: 'Little man, little man, the word must is not to be used to princes. If your father had lived, ye darest not have said so much.' At length she could no longer speak but signalled clearly her agreement to James' succession. When the Archbishop, who was praying beside her, started to move away the Queen made a small gesture for him to remain. At three in the morning of the 24th March, 1603, the Queen was seen to be dead.

TWO KINGDOMS ONE

Two kingdoms one: My end may do some good.
*   We progress much: tire not. I like the name*
I chose: all deign to praise me, as they should.
*   Great Britain: Thus to England her new name!*

Let music play. Time has her whim and I
*   My Tudor Rose, whose petals fall on Stuart earth.*
Shall James profane these courts through which dance I?
*   Leaves dance in Autumn air. Who counts their worth?*

Bring me my men who sadly dream too far:
*   Increase our pension to my Scottish heir.*
The oracles are wise: Pay well the star
*   That waits. It is, I think, my time for prayer.*

Wait no more: wave one old Queen away.
Two kingdoms one, remember that; and pray.

– 1603 –

The Picture Gallery

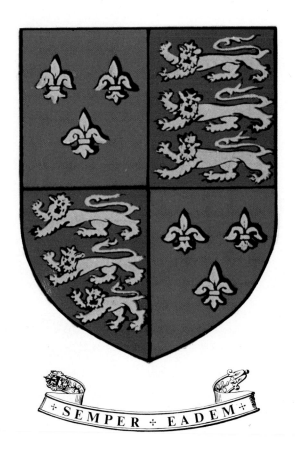

+ SEMPER + EADEM +

Elizabeth I as Princess

Thomas Seymour

Henry VIII

Anne Boleyn

Lady Jane Grey
Attrib. Master John c 1545

Mary I
Sir Antonio More

Launch
Arm

s on the
elines

Sir John Hawkins

Robert Dudley,
First Earl of Leicester c 1575

First Baron Burghley
Attrib. A. van Brounckhorst
c 1560–70

Mary, Queen of Scots
After N. Hilliard

Robert Devereux,
Second Earl of Essex *c 1597*

Robert Cecil,
First Earl of Salisbury
J. de Critz the Elder 1602

Elizabeth I
*Master of the Darnley
Face Mask circa* 1600